AF472293

A Lifetime of Words

Spirit for the Soul

By Robin Gorley

Second Printing

Dedication

This book is dedicated to all who seek the Lord and need His healing touch, and for those who know their Lord and Savior.
To the two Spiritual Leaders in my life, Pastor Wayne Weissenbuhler, who through most of my childhood was my mentor and guided me through the death of my father.
Your constant presence in my life has always meant more to me then words could ever say.
Pastor Rick Bloom, whose sermons has given me a new spiritual release and helping me to get to know my Lord and Savior in a more intimate way. Your words are healing, and I am forever grateful for your strong belief in the Lord.

Acknowledgments

To my Lord and Savior for being a constant presence
in my life and that of my family's life.
You are my rock and salvation and for that I am grateful.

Introduction

This installment of my series A Lifetime of Words, are words that are for those who need a spiritual touch in their life. My goal here is to touch your soul with words that God has given me to share with you. I love writing spiritual poetry. When I write poetry about God, I truly feel that He is speaking to me, through me. His strong presence reigns down on me as I write. Spirit For The Soul is one of my favorites; I guess it is because I truly believe that God is my Savior and that I know that He is always a part of my life. Some of my poetry will be from my first book A Lifetime of Words, *a*nd there will be some new poems as well.

There is a song that I love and it really sums things up for me. The song is by Kathy Troccoli and the title of this song is "My Life Is in Your Hands." The words of this song are so powerful and so true that you can't help but know that your life is ultimately in the hands of God.

8

My life is in Your hands
My heart is in Your keeping
I'm never without hope
Not when my future is with You.
My life is in Your hands
And though I may not see clearly,
I will lift my voice and sing,
'Cause Your love does amazing things.
Lord, I know my life is in Your hands.

It does not matter whether you believe or not, and I am not here to tell you if there is a God or not. What I am here to say is that my words are from my soul, the soul God has given me, and He wants me to tell the world. With that being said, after reading A Lifetime of Words: Spirit for the Soul, it will ultimately be your decision.

Albert Einstein once said, “I want to know God’s thoughts; the rest are details.”

I believe that without God’s thoughts, we wouldn’t be.

Enjoy the book!

Poetically,
Robin Gorley

More Than We Can Bear

It has been a known thought
To many of us,
That God does not send
More than we can bear.
Our hearts will mend
After the storm has passed,
As long as we keep God in our heart.
God holds us in His palm.
Love, faith and trust make us one,
Even though there are days that
Bring pain and
The burden of life's trials,
We must have faith in His ways.
We will triumph once the fear has passed.
God tells us to pray and to remember to love,
Because it will make us stronger
To know that God is always near,
To help us,
To guide us,
To give us strength whenever we are weak.

By Your Side An Angel

When you are hurt, or about to face
The unbearable,
May you know that by your side,
There is an angel.
When you need encouragement
For your dreams,
Inspiration to bring you happiness,
May you know that by your side,
There is an angel.
When tears replace smiles
Along those roads,
Then you truly are beginning to know
That by your side,
There is an angel.
When your disappointments turn to joy,
When clouds show you rainbows,
Then you know
That there is an angel
By your side.

A Prayer For Parents

Heavenly Father, I come to You
To ask for Your help.
I want to be a better parent.
I need You to teach me
So that I may understand my children.
I need to listen patiently to what they
Have to say,
And answer their questions
With understanding,
To keep from interrupting when they are trying
To explain what is on their mind.
Show me how to give them the
Words that would help them
To make the right choices.
Help me to discipline with love
And not give in when I need to be strong.
I ask that You help me to be fair, just, kind and fit,
And let them know that I will always love them,
No matter what they have done or said.
Amen.

Strength vs. Courage

Strength to fit in,
To feel the pain of others,
Hiding your own pain,
Endurance.
To stand alone,
To love others,
That is strength.
Courage to stand out,
Feel your own pain,
To show that you are not
As weak as you seem.
To stop when you
Can't take it anymore.
To be loved,
And to live life
As God would want you to,
That is courage.

Faith, Our Gift from God

From my heart to yours,
I believe that the world
We are in today,
Is our temporary setting.
For God has asked us to believe
And that we must not let our faith go away.
Faith is our gift from God.
He has given us this gift so that we
May know that a new world waits.
He asks us to be faithful, to trust in His word.
I believe that the path I am treading
Shall come safely through
The dangers I'm dreading,
And some day I will be sharing
In His infinite plan.
To one day with the Wisest,
The Master is serving Faith,
Our gift from God.

A New Found Strength

There are times in my life
When I feel hurt and alone.
But I believe that these are times
When I also feel lost and afraid.
All around me
I feel like things are falling apart,
The bridges of growth
I struggle to recapture.
That insecure feeling of
Not feeling secure.
But in spite of it all,
I emerge to something
Grander.
A newfound strength,
A new awareness.
It is almost as if
I must go through this
Pain and struggle to grow,
And to have a newfound strength.

God Said No

I was sitting in my chair,
Depressed as usual.
I decided to pray and ask God
To take my pain away,
But to my surprise, God said no.
I asked God to help me with my
Disabilities, to make me whole,
But to my surprise, God said no.
I asked God to help me to be
Patient with myself and others,
But to my surprise, God said no.
I asked God for happiness
To help make my spirit grow,
That I might enjoy life
And love others just like He loves me.
But to my surprise, God said no

What was God telling me?
Pain is not for me to take away or to give up
Although my spirit is whole,
My body is only temporary.
Patience is a by-product of
Trials and tribulations,
It is granted; it is earned.
God gives us blessings,
Happiness is all up to you.
Suffering can only draw you apart
From the cares of the world,
Only to bring you closer to Him.
God says, we need to grow on our own,
But He will prune you to make you fruitful.
God gives us life so that we can enjoy all things.
When asking God to help me love others,
That is when I truly knew what He meant.
God never really said no,
He just said be true to yourself and have faith.

A Better Place

A better place
Is what is waiting,
A place to walk
Near the clear blue waters.
Where it is known
A mansion for all,
Our Lord and Savior
With a burning passion.
Has God Finished
All that He has
Asked of me?
Maybe so—-
I'm walking on streets of gold.
God's Holy light
Fills the night.
Oh, please let me
Hear Him tonight.
A better place
Is what is waiting,
A place to walk
Near the clear blue waters.

Music of Angels

A choir singer I may be,
Struggling to find the
Difficult note.
A human voice
That fails more than prevails.
Will I ever have a voice worthy
To reach Heaven's gates?
To join the music of Angels
In the strains of eternal love?

Closeness To God

Closeness to God
For all who call,
When you begin to fall
God is there.
A prayer to Him
Could draw Him closer,
No matter how long or how far.
A kind touch to those
Who don't know
The closeness to God.
A love that is as deep as the
Ocean floor,
A heart as wide as
The valley low,
A power so powerful,
A gift every hour.

The Many Gardens of God

The lily stands for purity.
Our hearts should also be like a lily,
A pure and true lily,
As are the many gardens of God.
The rose stands for love.
A symbol if you will
Of God's love,
A fragrance for God's pure heart,
As are the many gardens of God.
The violets are strong in faith.
Abides steadfast and true.
Our life in God's hands,
As are the many gardens of God.
The pansy a sign of friendship.
With kindness and grace.
Teaching us so that we
May gather at His feet,
As are the many gardens of God.
The daisy, wisdom,
Which comes from the heart,
God's compassion,
Hope from above,
Hope for all,
As are the many gardens of God.

Jesus, The Messiah

He has been known to be the
Miracle man.
We have read of these miracles
Through the word.
Miracles are not
His only task.
He teaches,
He gives love,
He gave of Himself,
By giving His life.
Jesus, the Messiah,
He alone is a miracle of life.

I Saw An Angel

When I was young
I often looked for angels.
Never seeing one personally
It peaked my curiosity.
When I was young
I remember lying on the grass.
Looking up at the sky watching
Clouds go by.
Did I see an Angel
Sitting on a cloud?
Somewhere out there
I know there are Angels.
No matter if they are on
A cloud, in the sky,
Or beside me.

The Look of a Guardian Angel

Have you ever wondered
What a Guardian Angel
May look like?
Will this Guardian Angel
Be male or female?
Will this Guardian Angel
Have wings as white
As a dove on their back?
A gentle touch of love,
A soft hand when they touch,
Hair as gold as the streets of heaven,
Lips as red as a rose,
Eyes that see your
Every need, every worry,
A voice that sings
And offers peace of mind.
Will they wear long white gowns,
And have a halo
That shines bright in the night sky?
A Guardian Angel,
A symbol of God.

Blessings From The Lord

I want to thank my
Lord and Savior for giving me so
Many blessings even
When I don't deserve it.
His caring heart is never far from me
I know He is near always.
I want to thank my Lord and Savior
For being my best friend,
When others would walk away.
I never have to worry whom to talk to,
Because I know
He is near always.
I want to thank my
Lord and Savior for being
There always.
For the tough times,
And the good times,
He is near always.
I want to thank my
Lord and Savior for
Everything He has given me.
My family, my husband, my son.
For giving me life and reminding me
Everyday that this life is only temporary,
For He has told me,
We have a better place to go.
Thank you Lord, for giving me
Strength everyday,
For allowing me to continue
To do Your work,
Because I am always near
To You because of You.

My Father Please Forgive Me

I ask Father
For Your forgiveness,
For I am a sinner.
I need to know You are by my side,
To help me to be better,
To do Your work.
I only ask that You forgive me.
I know that I've done
Wrong—
I want to do right.
I'm truly sorry for not being
All that I can be.
I know I should never hide
From Your glorious light.
I pray for forgiveness,
For I am a sinner.

Are You Here Lord?

I ask the Lord
"Are You here?"
The Lord replies
"Yes, I'm always here."
When you are in need,
When you need someone to talk to you,
When you are feeling frustrated,
When you are feeling sad and unwanted,
All you have to do is
Call on Him.
For the Lord is here,
Always and Forever!

My Friend Is…

I have a friend
Who is very special and
Dear to my heart.
He is a friend to many,
But for some,
He is often turned away.
I met this friend
Many years ago,
When I was a child.
It was through a book
That I met this Man,
Words that are so sacred and true.
My friend has taught me much.
He has taught me to love, forgive,
To pray for whatever is on my mind.
I can ask for help and can be
Rest assured that I would get an answer,
Even if the answer really
Wasn't what I wanted.
He taught me to listen to others,
To myself and especially to Him.
He has taught me to
Trust Him and only Him.
But most of all He has taught me
To love without pretense.
29
My friend is my
Heavenly Father,
The creator of all things.
I am glad that He is my friend.

Pathway

Cheerfully I walk along
The pathway,
Faithfully asking, knocking
And seeking,
To fulfill the longing desire
That stirs deep in my soul.
Turning steadily to the word,
Gleaning the hidden truths,
Receiving without measure,
God's promised words.
Lovingly, God has challenged me,
Within my heart,
Seeking His spiritual touch,
Helping deal with the ways
Of the world,
Only wanting God's approval.
Dedicated,
To hold onto the word of God,
Which empowers our souls
And the spirit of man.
31
Come forth from
God's word,
As you flourish spiritual growth.
Lights casting forth,
Touching others throughout
The world.
Only with the hope of Heaven
Capturing life, and God's character.

Our Time is Short

Our time is short,
It is a time to be strong
In what you believe.
Our time is short,
Between now and then
Your faith must be strong.
Our time is short,
Learn to fasten your tongue
For time is not to waste.
Our time is short,
Time to make things right.
No excuses,
We are no longer sinners.
Our time is short,
Demons will arrive.
Stand strong,
You must keep the
Spirit alive.
33
Our time is short,
You know by now.
Keep yourself true
To our Lord and Savior.
For He knows
Our time is not only short,
But it is coming soon!

God of All

The sun will shine,
The wind blows,
Day and night,
Comes and goes.
The seed of human kind
Only to sow.
Always guarding
The harp and strings,
All that nature brings,
The Heavens in one accord.
God of all,
Being of supremacy.
The life that pushes on,
Only to find strength
In the heart and soul.
For me,
You are Lord of All!

It Was Once Said

Someone once said
That you can live
Life without love.
Living without love,
Is telling God
You don’t trust.
Life without love
Is for the dying.
Living but not loving,
Is not the way to live.

The Heavens Are Lined With Gold

If Heaven is for the young at heart,
Then it must be a child
To lead the way.
Games and ice-cream cones
Are found where Angels play.
Clowns, carousels and ponies,
Bloom with bright rainbows.
A child's laugh touches the stars,
So darkness might have light.
Heaven's streets of gold,
Jewels of jade and ruby,
Line up along each side.
No fear tonight,
Cause darkness never comes,
For Heaven's lights shine brighter,
Then any moon or star.
The mansion sits upon the hill,
No walls, just love.
Dreams once gone
Stand tall and proud,
Complete and perfect.
Someday we will one day
Wake only to find,
That there is
No more sin.
I take the hands of those I've loved,
Only to laugh, play and give a hug.

The Heavens

Almighty is my God,
My light...
Looking toward the heavens,
A glow...
Prayer the all important
Day and night...
Asking to receive
All the love He bestows.
Ignoring...
Not an option,
Wrong...
Right only He can say.
My faith, my heart...
Reign down upon me.
Your wisdom, knowledge,
And insight is all I need,
Never to forget what
I all ready know.

My Heart-Uncharted Path

My heart has an uncharted path.
It sometimes echoes
Deep inside,
A piercing wind,
Sharp.
Some left to feel
A joy of unheard song.
The heart unable to anchor,
An uncharted path
With no direction.
Give me the direction
God knows,
He has sat the path
I must wait.

Shine Upon Me

The Heavens open,
The light shines.
It is the Angels that
Shine upon me.
Heaven's hope,
Bless me with
Your wisdom.
Protect my soul,
Your light,
The only defense.
Guide and give direction.
Strengthen me,
Enlighten my soul.
Your vision-
My vision.
Help me to embrace the light
That shines upon me.

To Become a Child of God

Overjoyed with this new believer the missionary,
Went and bought her a new white dress.
Anxious to see her at the church, the missionary
Saw she was nowhere to be found.
Concerned, the Missionary traveled to her home.
Upon arriving at her home he found her lying in the dirt,
Her dress torn, filthy and soaked in blood.
The missionary discovered that her father did not share
In her joy and her new found faith.
With a heated rage her father had
Beaten her and left her to die.
The missionary carefully picks her up,
Carried her back to church,
And got the doctor to come and help her.
Unfortunately, it was too late.
This young girl dies from her severe injuries,
All because she found the Lord.
Before she died, she woke up and told the missionary,
That in spite of what happened she forgave her father for
What he had done, and that her prayer was that God
Would forgive him, so that
Her father would find the Lord.
A Child's love,
One of God's greatest gifts.

God Does Answer Prayer

I know not by what method rare,
But this I know...
God Answers Prayer.
I know that He has given His word,
This tells me prayer is always heard.
God Answers Prayer.
So I pray and calmly wait.
I know not if the blessing sought
Will come in just the way I thought.
But leave my prayers with Him alone,
Whose will is wiser than my own.
Assured that He will grant my request,
Or send some answer far more blessed.
God Answers Prayer.

The Heaven's Tears

Watching as the snow falls,
As the wind blows,
A story that my father and mother
Once told me long ago.
A reflection upon their words,
My mind brought back in time,
Lessons they taught
About life's journey.
My father says to me that
When it rains and the thunder roars,
It is God and Satan fighting.
Who will win?
My father tells me, "God always wins."
Some say it may be that the rain
Is Heaven's Tears,
God's saving hand.

The Name in the Sand

I walk alone on the ocean coast,
A pearly shell was at my feet.
I bent down to pick the shell up
When I saw something strange.
What was it that I saw?
It was a name, but a name
That you don't see often enough.
This name in the sand
Was God.
But it just wasn't the name God
That caught my eye,
It was the way it was written.
There was a light, a glow in the sand,
Not like when you write in the sand
And you just have sand,
This name was engraved in the sand.
After examining the writing
I looked up,
There was a shadow,
Another light, another glow.
It was God and He spoke to me,
Telling me that He wrote
His name in the sand,
And that I must do the same.

Songs of Rejoicing

Songs of rejoicing,
Of love and of cheer,
Are the songs that I'm yearning for,
Year after year.
The songs about children,
Who laugh with glee,
Are the songs worth singing,
A bright song for me.
Songs of rejoicing,
Of kisses and love,
Of faith in the Father,
Who sends from above,
The sunbeams to scatter,
The gloom and the fear,
These songs worth singing,
The songs of cheer.
Songs of rejoicing,
Oh, sing them again,
The brave songs of courage,
Appealing to all.
Of hope in the future of heaven,
The songs of rejoicing,
That strengthens the soul,
That is the goal.

God Has Days

There are two days in the week,
Upon which and about I never worry.
Two carefree days kept sacredly
Free from fear and apprehension.
One of these days is yesterday.
Yesterday, with its cares, frets, pains, aches,
All its faults, its mistakes and blunders,
Has passed forever beyond my recall.
It is mine; it is God's.
Tomorrow, with all its possible adversities,
Its burdens, its perils,
Its large promise and performance,
Its failures and mistakes,
Is as far beyond my mastery,
As its not here yet.
Tomorrow is God's day,
It will also be mine.

The Mansion

The mansion sits upon
The hill,
No walls, just love.
Dreams once gone,
Stand tall and proud,
Complete and perfect.
Someday we'll one day,
Wake only to find,
That there is
No more sin.
I take the hands of
Those I've loved,
Only to laugh, play
And give a hug.
The mansion sits upon the hill
Where I meet my creator.

The Challenges of God

Cheerfully I walk along
The pathway,
Faithfully asking, knocking,
And seeking,
To full-fill the longing desire
That stirs deep in my soul.
Turning steadily to the word,
Gleaning the hidden truths
Receiving without measure,
God's promised words.
Lovingly, God challenges me within,
Seeking His spiritual touch,
Helping deal with the ways
Of the world,
Only wanting God's approval.
Dedicated to hold onto the word of God,
Which can empower our souls
And the spirit of man.
Come forth from
God's word,
As you flourish spiritually.
Lights casting forth,
Touching others
Throughout the world.
Only with the hope of heaven
Capturing life,
And the character of God.

In the Name of Jesus Pray!

When you are weak,
Not sure which direction
You need to go,
Then in the name of Jesus,
Pray!
Satan will hear
Your prayer,
But Jesus will
Prevail!
Under no circumstance
Must you let Satan win!
Satan likes it when
We are vulnerable,
That is when he strikes.
When you are feeling weak,
Then by all means,
In the name of Jesus,
Pray!

There-The Angel On My Shoulder

As I was praying
I felt something
On my shoulder,
There, on my shoulder
The angel.
I wished that I could
Know this angel,
To feel this angel
In my hands.
To hear her voice,
Whispering in my ear.
There, the angel
On my shoulder,
Never to leave my side,
Watching over me tenderly,
The angel on my shoulder.

Touched by an Angel

Someone once told me
That I was
Touched by an angel.
They said that
My face
Glowed when I spoke.
When someone
Was hurting
And in pain,
They saw how
I comforted them.
I don't know if
I have been touched by an angel,
But I do know
I have been touched
By God.

Faith, Hope, Love

Faith, hope, and love,
Are the three things
God has given us.
Faith,
God has faith in us,
We must have faith in Him.
Hope,
God gave us hope,
So we could look towards something.
We must have hope
In that God will soon
Come to save us.
Love,
God gave us love
To express ourselves to each other.
We must remember
That God loves us,
We need to love Him back!
Faith, hope and love,
The three most powerful
Words God has given us.

God Walks beside You

When life's road seems
Dark and foreboding,
And the hills too steep to climb,
And you just know you're
Going to stumble,
It is only a matter of time.
Don't ever stop walking, just slow down,
And you'll find some time each day
To enjoy the countless wonders
God has place along the way.
If the going ever gets too tough,
And you really could use a friend,
Remember God walks beside you,
As He will, till your journey's end.
Just reach out and call His name,
He'll guide you and protect you,
And help you understand,
That life is never easy.
There will be joy and sorrow,
But if you learn to turn to Him,
He'll get you through each tomorrow.

A Child's Love

An unknown child stood
Outside the doorway
Of the church,
Intrigued by those inside.
A missionary had asked her to
Come in but she was afraid to.
It wasn't that she didn't want to,
In fact it was quite the opposite,
Her heart was beckoning to join in
On the singing and worshipping.
She'd seen how happy they all were,
The fellowship was so spontaneous and natural.
But where this little girl came from,
Worshipping the Lord in this manner,
Was not allowed.
She wasn't even allowed to have
Anything to do with Christians.
Unknown to this little girl,
The missionary began praying fervently for her soul,
Longing for the day when she could join them inside,
To learn of Jesus and how His blood was
Shed for her sins.
Every week the young girl would find herself
Standing at the church door.
She had a strange feeling
Like something was happening and drawing
Her to this church.
Each week that she would show up,
She found it harder to walk away.
One Sunday morning,
The young girl decided this was the time
She was going to accept the missionary's invitation to come
to the church.
After a few weeks this young girl
Opened her heart to Jesus.

God's World

Oh world, I cannot hold you close enough!
The winds, they are wide with gray skies.
The mists that roll and rise,
The woods, this autumn day,
That aches and sags,
And all but cry with color,
I cannot get close enough!
Long have I known a glory in it all,
But never knew this.
Here such a passion,
Is as though it was stretching me apart Lord.
I do fear that the world is too beautiful,
My soul is all but out of me—
Let fall no burning leaf;
Let no bird call.

A Bouquet from Heaven

May each day unfold for you,
Like roses, sparkling with dew,
That opens to the morning sun,
And bloom until the day is done.
And may each passing moment bring,
A song as pure as angels sing.
But may there be above all things,
A peace that only God can bring.

God Loves a Cheerful Giver

There's no sense in giving
If not from the heart,
For that is where loving
And giving both start.
There's no need for sharing
If it's not true,
That your reason for sharing
Is because you want to.
If you're going to give
Then do it because,
The gift comes from the heart
Overflowing with love.

Our Hearts

Together our hearts beat a rich harmonic
Song of the joyous love we share.
A love beyond words that only
Two hearts can sing.
It is the first breath of a newborn baby,
Cradled in his mother's arms,
As they gaze for the first time
Into each other's eyes.
It is the life giving warmth from the sun,
Which is upon the wings of a butterfly
As it struggles for its first flight on a
Spring morning.
It is the way we feel
As we look into the heavens
On a warm clear night,
When the stars shine,
And admire God's
Miraculous creations.
It is the humbleness we feel
And the sanctity we enjoy.
Because it's God's goodness,
Power and love
That gives us our hearts.

He Cares

Can we walk among the lilies,
And still not be aware,
As we behold their royal robes,
That somehow, God cares?
Does He not feed the sparrow,
And bathe the rose with dew?
If He then watches over them,
Think how much He cares for you.

A Prayer

We all have many prayers,
Many that need answers,
And many that have no answers.
We all need to be patient and kind,
And remember that the prayers
Will be answered,
It is just a matter of time.
God knows what He is doing.
Don't fret your turn is coming,
Give Him a break.
What does your prayer mean?
What do you need?
God is coming don't you cry,
Wipe your tears dry,
God is on His way.
God has answered,
Now you may pray to thank Him.
Don't forget, God has more to get.

God’s Rainbow Has Tears

What a collection the Lord has,
Bottles lined up in a row.
Upon each bottle there is a name,
But who’s, may we ask?
And in that bottle we see tears,
Where do they come from, may we ask?
“My child,” God says, these are tears
Of joy, tears of grief, tears of laughter,
And tears of love.
Soon the bottle will be full,
Maybe overflowing.
So what do you do
With these bottles, may I ask?
I take them and sprinkle
Them down from the
Heavens as it is needed,
To help with emotions.
And in each dose that is given out,
I the Lord of Lords,
Pour my special ingredients into each bottle.
This gives us just what is needed to make
A rainbow of tears.

My Prayer

Looking toward the east,
As the sun comes out,
As I see beauty can do no wrong,
I pray to my God above to give me
The love I need,
To be faithful at all times,
In all places.
For I know I need forgiveness
For the wrongs I've done.
But I know He'll make me strong,
Because He loves me and I love Him.
Because of the love that
He shines upon me,
I find my life can stand still.
Now this is my prayer...I hope you hear,
Thank you for remembering
That I must keep it inside,
For I will never forget,
And no matter where I am,
I will love you for eternity.
Amen.

My Lord, I Know You're Here

My Lord is here,
I know He's doing His job.
When I need Him,
I just call on Him and
He comes a calling.
Never to fear when you
Are sad and blue,
Cause He'll know just what to do.
Just let Him know,
What trouble might be,
Because He is here,
I feel Him near.
In all I see and do,
I know He'll be here,
To think and to know
That He knows we care
Will bring Him here.
We know He's here
So just call on Him now,
Call Him soon,
Cause you know
He'll be here soon.
Yes, my Lord,
I know you're here.

Hear My Prayer

Now I lay me down to sleep,
I pray to the Lord
My soul to take.
If I should die before I wake
I pray to the Lord my soul is pure.
I ask every morning and night
For guidance and a still mind.
To give me His divine will,
Serenity still.
I start a new life,
Each with a new lesson,
Knowing that God keeps
His promises,
No matter what.
I know in my heart,
He keeps me close
To Him.
With humble souls,
And thankful times,
When I know I've done wrong,
I know He'll forgive,
I am grateful.
67
The power within His Holy Grace,
Rises above my saddened face.
Home at last,
Where kind, loving, gentle
And strong are all that is needed.
Home is where I belong.
May I know honesty and truth
From this point on.
Until that day comes,
I will have to deal with humility,
For purity and gratitude
Has to be earned.
God has found my humble heart
So now my spirit won't depart.

So on my knees I go,
To say my prayer,
To thank the Lord,
To lead me right.
Watch and keep me safe,
As I pray that I may live
To give.

The Journey of Life

There is a journey that I must face,
Filled with the things I have learned,
But I have to see.
As the tears fill up with anguish and pain,
I'm sorry that it is upon you.
There will be a sting, for the pain we feel.
But within our souls we will agree,
That we must all see that there
Will always be, times of pain.
But for now we must
Live in harmony,
And embrace all that we can.
Learn to be patient and kind,
But most of all,
We must be understanding.
Once again the journey of life begins.
No time,
Can't be late,
You know you can relate,
No regrets, just pain.

We had the chance, and let it by,
Our souls will fill up with love.
Giving time to understand,
That our paths are not different.
When we walk on God's land reach out,
Don't hold back, its okay.
This land is for the living,
Maybe its' not what we're use to,
But remember,
Life is for the living.
Living in God's world that is,
So don't sacrifice, but be forgiving.
As we go on our journey of life,
We will forgive ourselves and the others too.
Allowing for God's nurturing, spiritual health,
Moving on our journey of life.

Embrace Me, Lord

Embrace me, Lord,
For my life is in your hands.
Touch me, Lord,
For my life is in your hands.
Heal me, Lord,
For my life is in your hands.
Reign on me, Lord,
For my life is in your hands.
Breathe on me, Lord,
For my life is in your hands.
Embrace me, Lord,
So that I can embrace you.

A Purpose

Have you ever once asked yourself,
"What on earth am I doing here?"
We all have some kind
Of purpose on this earth.
It's not to hurt others
Or tell them their worth.
Everyone was put here for a reason.
Take a look around you,
Take a good long glance.
God has a purpose for all of us.
Some are here to teach, to heal,
Some are here to build,
And some to reach.
You may not know your purpose,
But God knows,
And He will tell you when
He knows you are ready.
It has all been planned
God will always be there to lend a hand.
Tough times, good times,
He has a purpose,
And so do you.

Live for today,
Live for God,
For when you do,
God will find your purpose,
And He will tell you,
That I am sure of.

Life Alone

I live alone, my dear Father
Stay by my side.
In all my daily strife's
Be my guide.
Grant me my desires
As you see fit.
Keep my mind pure,
My thoughts unselfish.
Hear my calling Lord
For I am feeling low.
I live alone, my dear Father.
But when I know You are near,
I am not alone evermore.

My Prayer for Renewal

Heavenly Father,
I am Your sheep...
Who needs healing.
I need Your cleansing touch,
For I am soiled
And cold.
Help me to know
Your love Father,
Through Your son
Jesus,
And through Your
Spirit.
Help me to love
And to show it.
As pure as the dove
That flies in the sky.
Help me to believe
In the mighty strength
Of Your words.
To hope joyfully
And love divinely.
Renew my faith Lord.
Amen.

A New Strength

There are times in our life
When we feel hurt and alone,
When we feel lost
And all around us we
Seem to be falling apart.
I ask myself,
Are these bridges of growth?
We struggle and try
To do what we can to recapture
The security that we once had.
We emerge on the other side
With a new understanding,
A new awareness,
A new strength.
Though it is almost
As if we must go through pain,
And we struggle
To grow,
And reach
A new strength.

Let Me Hear Your Voice

It has been one of those days Lord.
As I go about my daily chores,
Please...
Let me hear Your still small voice.
I know You will.
Because I love You,
I want to
Follow Your lead.
Guide me I pray,
Calm me,
Remind me.
Don't let me go ahead of You,
Lead me.
Thank you Lord,
For staying near me,
And guiding me
With Your still,
Calming voice.

I Shall Not Want

I shall not want
What You
Don’t want me
To have,
For You know Lord,
What I truly need.

The Hope We Have

Blessed is the hope
We have within us,
To anchor our soul
Steadfast and sure.
I found it in the promises
Of my Father's written word.
The hope we have is within our souls,
Brighter than any day.
God has given us His spirit.
I want the world to hear it.
All doubts gone away for the hope we have.

You Are Our Hope

Hope that is nearly gone Lord,
Reaching down
To the lowest,
Completely cast down.
At times feeling
Everything is hopeless,
Your word assures
Us that nothing
Is impossible,
When we put
Our trust in You.
Our life is in Your hands.
You are our hope
For eternity.

My Unsearchable Riches

Life is not about being rich,
It is about our
Unsearchable riches in Christ.
Wealth that can never be told,
Riches exhaustless
Of His mercy and grace,
It is more precious than gold,
More precious than silver.
Our Heavenly Father
Has taken care of
Those unsearchable riches,
By giving us His word!

Can It Be, The Lord Is My Sheppard?

My soul cries out
For the Lord to
Restore me again.
Give me strength
That has been taken away.
Show me the path to
Righteousness,
In the name
Of the Almighty God.
Yes, I see it now,
Lord, You are my Sheppard,
And You will lead me out of darkness.
Stand beside me in the still waters,
Quench my thirst,
Renew my soul.

The River of Peace

River of Peace
Feed my soul,
Make me perfect
And whole.
Increase the
Flow of Your blessings.
Let it be deep in
My soul.

Taking Care

Do not be dismayed
God will care for you,
Beneath His wings
You will abide,
For God will care for you.
Through each day,
Completely,
He will care for you.
No matter what,
God will care for you.
Lean on Him,
Never stray,
Because God is taking care
In your daily walk.

Trust Him Completely

All my fears
My weary soul,
The dark clouds that loom,
I must give to Jesus!
His light will never
Grow dim.
All I am,
Body, mind and soul,
I must give to Jesus!
Trust in Him completely,
Is what I have to hope for.
Because He has promised me,
Eternal life.

The Waiting

I pray to You
For answers;
You tell me to wait.
Why, must I wait
Dear Lord?
I am in trouble Lord,
You know that.
Why, must I wait
Dear Lord?
Give me patience I pray for.
I realize Your timing and
Wisdom is perfect.
I believe in You,
I trust in You,
I must wait.
Because I know
That waiting
Is just a part
Of whom You are,
And what you expect from me.

What God Promised

Don't forget
The promises God
Has made.
Never doubt why,
The road is smooth and wide,
Swift, and easy to travel
Not needing a guide.
Never doubt why,
The mountain rocky and steep,
A river turbid and deep.
What God has promised
Is strength for the day,
Rest for your tired soul,
A light to shine the way.
What God has promised
Is grace for the trials,
Help from above,
Unfailing sympathy,
His undying love.

Don't Forget to Pass on a Smile

Don't forget to pass on a smile
To someone that is disabled,
Someone who may have needs
That are unspoken.
Don't forget to pass on a smile
To someone who asks
For a little prayer,
For a friendly hand.
Just a little smile
Is all that they may need.
And when you tell them,
That smile is from Jesus,
Maybe they will catch His ray.
Because bright smiles
Have filled the day,
Especially when they are
Smiles Jesus gave.
So don't forget
To pass a smile.

You're Wounds Are for Me

Your wounds are for me,
For the world.
You live for me,
Beside me.
Your prayers are
Daily pleading,
For Your wounds are for me.

Your Comfort Is But…

Your comfort
To bless,
Is but Thine own.
Your calm
Your touch,
Is but Thine own.
You tend to us,
You give to us,
Is but Thine own.
You are the comfort,
The Angel that works,
Is but Thine own.

The End of the Rope

I have reached the
End of the rope,
Struggling,
The strife,
The pain.
I can't hang on,
I will never gain.
I have reached the
End of the rope,
Suffering, overshadowing
Everything that is good.
Is there hope?
Yes, God is there,
At the end of
The rope.
I have reached the
End of the rope,
The load I cannot bear,
No strength to even try,
Seems no one cares.

I beg for strength,
To take away the
Aches and pains.
Is there hope?
Yes, God is there,
At the end of
The rope.
I now see
That the end of the rope,
Is not all bad.
God is there at the end
Of the rope.
Where He does His best work.
He has the answers,
I must let Him work out the rest.
My heart is renewed
With goals, dreams,
And changes.
I have found that at
The end of the rope,

God is there,
For eternity.

God's Faithfulness

There is a song in my
Heart that is known
To most.
It talks about God's Faithfulness,
And how He has provided
All that we need.
Morning by morning,
New mercies He gives.
Day by day
I see His mercies.
Great is His Faithfulness,
Great I will be
Because of His Faithfulness.

Give the Best Of Yourself to the Master

I give You my Lord,
The best I can possibly be.
I give You my strength,
My soul,
The soul that You made fresh.
For if it were not for You Master,
Giving the best of Yourself,
Would not be just to the Master,
But to myself.

The Blessings

in the Little Things

I find that in life,
Blessings come in many
Different sizes.
It doesn't matter whether they
Are big or little.
What matters is that
God has blessed them.
Thank you Lord,
For granting me
Your blessing,
And for taking care of those little things
That seemed not to matter.
I know that I have to work hard
To meet those needs,
But as long as I have You beside me,
Reminding me,
That the little things
Are just as important as the big things,
I will always stay within Your good graces.

The Tie That Binds You and I

Before I go to my Father's house,
I pour out prayers.
I tell him of my fears,
My hopes,
My dreams.
He comforts me by telling me,
That the ties that bind
You and I,
Are the ones He has written in the sky.

Please Lord, Hold My Hand

I ask but a simple request,
As danger surrounds us,
And the darkness envelops us,
Please Lord,
Hold my hand.
Your hand strong,
Will lead us to safety.
Your touch takes away the long weary hours,
No matter what they may be.
I ask but a simple request Lord,
Please hold my hand.

Let Me Walk With Thee

Let me walk with thee,
My dear Savior.
The path seems low.
Help me to bear
The strain of toil,
The fret of care.
Teach me the way Lord,
For I am homeward bound.
Teach me patience, to be still,
Let me come closer,
That I may keep the faith
Strong over any wrong
That may triumph,
And make me distrust.

Anoint Me

Anoint me Holy Spirit,
Bathe my trembling heart.
Fill me with Your
Hallowed presence.
Come, Holy Spirit,
Anoint me.
Touch my heart,
Comfort,
Bless me,
Save me.
For you are the
Anointed one.

I Will Go Where He Leads Me

I will go where
You lead me Lord.
You are calling me,
And I hear Your voice
In my ear.
I will go where
He leads me.
I will follow Him
Where ver He wants me to go.

God Uses Our Gifts

Although I don’t feel
That I am very talented,
Thank you Lord,
For calling me to use my gifts.
I understand
That You have work for me,
And I am willing
To use my
Gifts to Your glory.
I know I cannot tell You I can’t,
Because You know
That I can,
And I will not
Be disobedient
If I don’t.
So anoint me Lord,
Fill me with Your power,
Use me for Your Glory.

Thanks Lord, For Filling My Cup

In my quiet hour,
I sit and talk with You
My Lord.
Not anything in particular,
But things in life.
You listen immensely
With love and care.
I seek Your guidance
Through Your word,
As I prepare
For a new day.
Thanks Lord,
For filling my cup
Each and every day.
For overflowing my soul
With Your warm, loving Spirit.
Thank you for nourishing
My thirsty soul.

Behold, God's Love

Behold,
God's Love,
Boundless,
Never ending.
God loves us all
In-spite of our pitfalls.
Behold,
God's Love.

Your Boundless Love

Your boundless love
Frees me from all pain.
Anguish, sorrow, melt away
Wherever Thy healing arises.
Nothing may I see,
No desire must I seek,
Only Your boundless love.
Draw me nearer,
Shall I run to You?
To hear Your gracious words,
Comforting.
Your boundless love,
Never to fear.

Our Lord

The time has come Lord,
For Your mighty works,
Your wondrous grace.
For You are our Lord,
The one to proclaim,
In all the earth.
How glorious
Is Your name Lord!

His Soul Has Awakened, For He Lives!

My soul,
Awake to the joyful
Sounds of God's praises.
My Redeemer Lives!
As the song says.
When troubled times come calling,
When happy times commence,
Remember...
Thatyour soul has awakened,
For He Lives!

Jesus Shine On Us

His light so clear,
So pure,
A candle burning
In the night,
A world that is dark,
Must see Jesus
Shine on us.
In a corner,
In a hole,
Or in a quiet place,
All our own,
Jesus will shine on us
For eternity!

I Thank God For My Church

A place where I can go
To pray,
To sing His praises,
To console.
I thank God
For my church.
A place that is sacred,
His presence always felt.
Those who are around me,
I feel God.
For He has given me a church;
But more than a church,
He has given me His touch,
In a place that no one
Can take away from me...
My church.

The Sweetness of That Hour of Prayer

When I am in need,
Or when I just need to talk,
God says to just pray.
That sweet hour of prayer
I feel I must share,
With those whose
Spirits are anxious.
Even burning.
With a strong desire
For His return,
God my Savior shows me,
That prayer is our best tool.
I wait patiently
For the sweetness,
Of that hour of prayer.

Take Me to That Quiet Place

I ask You Father,
To take me to that quiet place.
The early morning walk,
The space in which I may think.
You have shown me how
To use my time.
You allow me to
Shine in that moment.
Take me to that
Quiet place, Father,
For You know my desires.
Thank you for Your blessings
As I bring my needs to You.
Thank you for allowing me to be me,
And giving me all that I need.
Take me to that quiet place Father.
The place where You
Continue to teach me to be
All the best that I can,
Through Your words,
Your thoughts,
And Your plan.

The Mysterious Ways Of God

People say that God moves
In mysterious ways.
I truly believe that He does.
His wonders all so real,
His footsteps along the sea,
I see them,
Riding upon the waters,
Through the storms.
Those who fear Him, take courage.
The clouds may be dark,
His mercy shall break,
As He lays blessings
On your shoulders.
You will then see
The mysterious ways
Of God.

The More I Pray, the Nearer You Feel

When I see the blue sky,
I know that a new day has begun,
I know that You are near.
When I begin my prayer,
And offer You praise,
I know You are near.
When life gets stressed,
And daily strife becomes unbearable,
I know You are near.
When things don't go right,
And I ask for Your help,
I know You are near.
When I see my family,
When my son gives me a hug
And tells me he loves me,
I know You are near.
As each moment passes,
Whatever it might be,
The more I pray,
The nearer You feel.

Don’t Forget the Little Things

So many times in life,
When we pray and ask for God
To answer our prayers,
We tend to forget the
Little things.
Searching for God’s blessings,
Even trying hard to find one,
Can cause you to walk in the shadows,
Hanging on for that one unanswered
Prayer.
Failing to see His wonders,
The ones that God
Offers to you each and every day.
What He bestows,
Is all the joy He sends your way.
So when you are praying,
Reading God’s words,
Don’t forget, that the
Little things are just
As important and the big things.

For the Little Things

I Thank You

I sometimes go along
Full speed if you will,
Not looking both ways.
I sometimes forget
To look to You,
For the little things.
So many things to accomplish
In just a few hours of the day.
And when I achieve that goal,
I forget to look to You,
For the little things.
So let me say,
“Thank you for the little things
That You give me each day.
Thank you for keeping me on my
Toes, and reminding me
That everything I do
In life is important,
No matter how big or how small.”

Jesus is Calling

Jesus is calling
On life's wild, restless, sea;
Day by day His sweet voice
Is saying,
"Christians, come home."
Jesus is calling
On the vain world in which we live;
Day by day His sweet voice
Is saying,
"Christians, come home."
Jesus is calling
Our joys and our sorrows;
Days of toil,
Still He calls us,
"Christians, come home."
Jesus is calling
By His mercies we must abide.
Will you hear Jesus calling,
Calling to have you come home?

The Solid Rock

When the trials, temptations,
Uncertainties, and anxieties,
Of our fast paced society beat us down,
Like that long walk, or that
Hurricane that takes us off our feet,
We can cling to the Solid Rock
Of Jesus Christ!

He's The Lover of My Soul

Lover of my soul,
Let me stand beside
The still waters
With You.
Take me Jesus,
To those still waters,
I trust You.
Reign down on me,
Make me pure in Your eyes,
Help me to see the truth.
Touch my soul Jesus,
For I have found
The Lover of My Soul.

When I Hear Beautiful Music

Thank you Lord,
For giving me
The ears to hear with,
The voice to sing,
The lips to move,
So that I may hear
Beautiful music.

Sheltering Presence

I am sheltered by Your presence,
You allow my soul to feel safe,
You teach me
As You keep me by Your side.
I am sheltered by Your presence,
Through the stress,
Through the turmoil,
You don't allow
It to destroy me,
No matter what the
Temptations might be.
I am sheltered by Your presence,
Where You welcome me
To come back to
Wherever I am in need.

A Time To Be Holy

A time to be holy,
Is to be with your Lord.
Abide in Him,
Feed on His word.
A time to be holy,
To make friends
With God's children.
Help the weak,
Forgetting nothing.
A time to be holy,
As the world rushes on.
Spend time in secret,
With Jesus along.
Look to Jesus,
His likeness you will see.
A time to be holy,
Let Him guide.
Do not run ahead of Him
Whatever you do.
Follow the Lord,
Keep your eye on Jesus,
Trust in His word.
A time to be holy,
Can calm the soul,
Every thought,
Beneath His control.
His Spirit
Over flowing with love,
Soon will be fitted,
For your time above.

Your Encouraging Presence

Concerns pile up around me,
Tired, frustrated,
And discouraged.
Sometimes I am at my wits end.
I pour out each worry to You,
I feel Your attentive,
Encouraging presence,
As only You know how to do.
You comforted my soul,
A peaceful feeling
Has blanketed me.
I feel your reassurance,
Perhaps someone
Was praying for me.
It amazes me always,
How in times of need
You always find a way
To show me,
That You are present.
The constant encouraging presence
Is all that I sometimes need.

I Like That You Think of Me

I like when You think of me,
Because I know that You love me,
In every instance of my life Lord.
Without a shadow of a doubt,
I am confident that You love me.
For all my insecurities,
As well as my gifts.
I always thought that
I had to prove something
By doing good for others,
In order to win Your love
And approval.
In some ways, I probably tried
To overachieve so I could gain
Appreciation and praise
From those who know me.
I was convinced that I would not be liked,
Especially if I slipped up in the least.
I thought I had to be perfect
Or I would lose Your love,
And the love of others.
Maybe I was teetering,
Putting myself on a pedestal.
Or maybe I just simply felt unworthy
Of a love that has always been there.
You took my insecurities and replaced
Them with assurance.
Your unwavering care and devotion,
Your merciful kindness.
I praise You for showing me
That You love me.
No matter the situation,
You have given me a sense of relief
From the strength that You have

Shown me.
You have calmed my weaknesses.
You have given me compassion
And forgiveness,
When I am not perfect,
And even when I am.

Trust In God

Trust in God,
For when you put your
Trust in Him,
He knows the way.
Having complete faith in God,
Is sometimes our most
Difficult and spiritual challenge.
Because of God's teaching,
His word and His
Constant nudging,
You learn to trust in
Him more.
By believing in God
With all of your heart,
With all of your soul,
God will show you the way.
By taking your concerns
To God,
You find that God has
Given you wise answers.
For when I try to handle
Things myself,
I tend to be impatient,
I mess things up,
I manage to be in the way.
But I am learning
To have faith,
In my prayers
And trust in God,
Unconditionally.
I have learned that when
I stand back and stay out of the way,
Allow you to do Your work,
I can stand and watch
Your miracles happen.
You not only taught me to trust,
You helped me become trustworthy.
You have shown me that when

I do step in,
Manipulate,
And try to fix things,
They are a lack of trust and
I am displeasing You.
I know this now, and I intend on
Trusting in You,
So that You will make
My paths straight.

How Close You Are

How close
You are,
My Lord,
When the evening falls,
Streaks of twilight
Linger over the darkness.
How close you are, my Lord,
Your voice I hear so clearly,
Your touch I feel so gently,
Your presence always near.

Book Reviews

Here is what others are saying about Robin's first book, A Lifetime of Words:

Robin Gorley's, A Lifetime of Words is just that. She has captured love, friendship, children, life mates, and everything in between through the pages of her book. I could read this book, over and over. Her feelings leap off the page as you read through her inspirational, uplifting and captivating words. They draw you in and allow you to feel what she feels. Robin does more than paint a picture with mere words; she gives us a peek into her heart, mind and spirit. Robin has given the reader the special gift of herself and her life experiences. A Lifetime of Words is a must for every poetry lover. It's the perfect gift and makes a great addition to any coffee table. It's bound to be a lasting conversation piece. **Terri Ann Armstrong, Author of My Soul Has Spoken and Where Do I Begin?** www.terrisheart.com

Deeply Written~ Jay Hurd Author-Ascension: Book One of The Alliance Chronicles, Steger, IL
Though I am not a fan of poetry, Robin's work is something that I consider very special. She blends humor with deep spirituality in a combination that is very easy to read, understand and leaves you feeling very good. She expresses her love of God in a simple, yet eloquent manner and teaches us God's love through her verse. Her collection of poetry spans 2 decades of her life and by reading what I have, I can tell you that it has been 2 decades well spent living in love and beauty. If you are in need of inspiration, know someone who is, or are looking for a gift for someone who shares Robin's deep love of God, then buy this book!

Lillian Brummet, co-author of Trash Talk Reviews; Canada
Her style is simple, using basic language and sometimes using common rhyming themes-yet she experiments with different styles of writing throughout the book. Several times, I was

forced to sit and contemplate what she wrote-not the entire poem, but sections stood out for me in a powerful way. Statements like “This is your day, warm and bright, each hour a gift...,” “My being is not a hindrance, but a blessing to move through life by chosen action...” and “When I walk alone, you will be the sun at my back and the smile on my lips...” were very moving for me.

A Lifetime Of Words~ Filled With A Host Of Enjoyable Pieces

Jesse Chavarria~ Editor of *Latino Today*

I like all kinds of poetry. I also like poetry that surprises me a bit, with an unexpected twist or turn. When I got a copy of Robin Gorley’s new poetry collection A Lifetime of Words I had doubts about whether it was the sort of poetry experience I could really appreciate. Robin is a local gal, extremely likable, caring and obviously gifted as a poet. The lavender-colored cover and swirled script title didn’t exactly say “rough” and “spirited” to me. Which goes to show that it’s better not to rush to judgment when it comes to poetry? I found that I really enjoyed the shorter pieces throughout the collection for their thoughtful quality.

www.ingramcontent.com/pod-product-compliance
Ingram Content Group UK Ltd.
Pitfield, Milton Keynes, MK11 3LW, UK
UKHW041935190726
13854UKWH00004B/1600

9 781387 229451